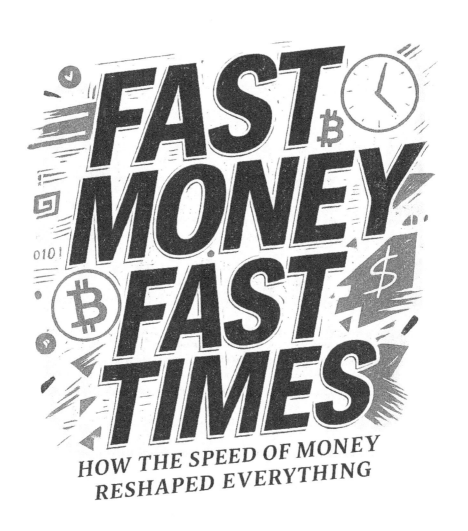

FAST MONEY FAST TIMES

HOW THE SPEED OF MONEY RESHAPED EVERYTHING

MAX MATLES, CFP®, EA

Copyright © 2025 by Max Matles

All rights reserved.

No part of this book may be reproduced, stored in a retrieval system, or transmitted in any form or by any means—electronic, mechanical, photocopying, recording, or otherwise—without the prior written permission of the publisher, except in the case of brief quotations embodied in critical articles or reviews.

First edition: 2025
Published by: **Matles Publishing**
MaxMatles.com

Disclaimer

This book is for informational and educational purposes only. It is not intended as legal, financial, investment, or tax advice. The author and publisher are not liable for any decisions made based on the contents of this book. Always consult a qualified professional before making any financial decisions.

ISBN: *979-8-89814-637-5*

Cover & Art Design by: *Juliana Garces-Echavarria*

Printed in the United States of America.

Acknowledgments

To Juliana: Thank you for your love, support, and for putting up with my endless thoughts and ideas.

To Jessie Nichols: Thank you for the books and ideas that sparked my imagination.

To my parents, Holly and David: Thank you for giving me the love, time, and space to grow. Parents like you are truly rare and make this world a better place.

                    With gratitude,
                            Max

Table of Contents

Author's Note: A Better Path Forward V

Introduction: What Happened to Time? 1

Chapter 1: The Speed of Everything 5

Chapter 2: The Sugar High 9

Chapter 3: Money, Gold, and Trust 13

Chapter 4: Fiat and the Fast Lane 19

Chapter 5: Build Fast, Break Faster 23

Chapter 6: Art Without Time 27

Chapter 7: War and Waste 33

Chapter 8: Bitcoin 39

Chapter 9: Visions of a Slower Future 47

Chapter 10: Choosing a Timeline 53

Chapter 11: The Cost of Now 57

Chapter 12: Teaching the Future 63

Chapter 13: The Final Goal 67

Author's Biography

Get in Touch with Max

Author's Note:
A Better Path Forward

Throughout history, the money that a civilization chooses, and the scarcity or abundance of that money has shaped nearly every aspect of life. We've used all kinds of things as money, often without questioning their value at the time. Seashells, glass beads, salt, tally sticks, silver coins, paper backed by gold, and now digital dollars created with a keystroke. From the stone wheels of Yap to the U.S. dollar and Chinese yuan, the definition of money has continually evolved. But each form has left its mark, shaping the way we trade, build, and think.

Money has influenced not just trade and wealth, but architecture, culture, art, music, education, family structures, and even the psychology of entire nations. Scarce money instilled care. Stable money fostered planning. When money held value, people built with the future in mind. When it didn't, urgency took over.

This book was born out of a desire to understand those patterns, not just in charts and policies, but in the rhythm of everyday life. To ask: what happens when time and money speed up, and what might happen if we choose to slow them down?

When I first began writing this book, I didn't intend to highlight any specific technology. But it's hard to talk about time, money, and sovereignty without acknowledging the rise of tools that challenge the entire foundation of life as we know it. Among them is Bitcoin, not just as a financial asset, but as an idea. A signal that something different is possible.

This isn't a Bitcoin pitch. I'm not interested in hype. What interests me is structure, and how certain tools reshape behavior. Decentralized systems like Bitcoin, by their nature, reintroduce scarcity and responsibility. They ask people to take ownership. To think further ahead. To slow down.

In some parts of the world, where inflation is rampant and institutions are unstable, Bitcoin has become more than just a speculative asset. It's become a way to preserve value. A tool for families to build continuity across generations. In those places, the long view isn't abstract. It's necessary.

That doesn't mean Bitcoin is right for everyone. And it doesn't mean technology alone will solve all of our modern problems. What matters most is the mindset. Whether it's through improved systems, better education, stronger communities, or new tools, the core question remains: Are we living in a way that respects and honors the future?

And if not, what will it take to start?

This book offers a vision for the future and holds a mirror up to our past. It is a reflection on where we've been, an idea of where we're headed, and explores what it means to reclaim time in a world that keeps speeding up.

May this book offer more than just a vision of a brighter future, may it present a moment to pause, reflect, and choose the best path. One built to last. And may it, in some small way, help bring greater peace to humanity and the world we share.

Introduction: What Happened to Time?

You used to have time. Time to sit, think, build, save, wait. Your parents had more of it. Your grandparents even more. And the deeper you go into history, the more patience and time people seemed to have.

They planted trees whose fruit they'd never eat. They built homes with stone and thick walls. They painted ceilings that took decades to finish.

Now we scroll, we ship overnight, we burn out, and we ask AI to do it faster. Somewhere along the way, we changed how we value time. Or rather, the incentives built into our money system, changed our perceptions of time and value.

This book is about what happened. Not just to time, but to meaning, culture, art, war, peace, and the invisible fuel that drives all of it: money.

You don't have to be an economist to feel something's off.

Everything feels rushed, disposable, and constantly replaceable. Products are intentionally made to wear out quickly or become outdated, so you'll have to buy them again. And that same mindset seeps into every part of human life, music, architecture, education, and even the way we connect with one another.

The root problem lies in the incentives of the money system we live in. A system that rewards speed over substance, volume over quality, urgency over care. It encourages us to act quickly, to move fast, to think short-term, at the expense of depth, durability, and future well-being.

It shows up everywhere.

In art designed to go viral one month and be forgotten the next. In music written by algorithms, for algorithms. In businesses built for an exit, not endurance.

It creates pressure. Pressure to do more, scroll more, consume more, without ever asking what any of it is really for.

There's a name for this mindset: **High Time Preference**. The tendency to favor now over later. Speed over patience.

And underneath it, as we'll explore, the major driving force is a money system that quietly encourages us to live faster, not better.

This is a book about choices, about what happens when we live in a world of Fast Times & Fast Money, and what becomes possible when we choose to slow them down again.

Chapter 1: The Speed of Everything

Imagine this: You wake up, roll over, and check your phone. Thirteen notifications. Two missed texts. One email that feels urgent but isn't.

You tap an app and a car is on its way. Coffee is already waiting at the next stop. You swipe, tap, scroll, swipe. You're absorbing the world in microseconds. It's efficient. It's convenient. It's kind of addicting. But it's not exactly enjoyable.

By 10:00 AM, you've been exposed to more stimuli than someone in the 1800s might encounter in their whole lives. You've already made dozens of small decisions, most without thinking. What to click. What to skip. What to like. What to buy.

Fast has become our default speed in every aspect of life. We don't question it. We just optimize it. And maybe that speed we feel is due to more than just technology advancing.

This book asks a simple question: What did we lose when everything sped up and how did that happen?

Because what looks like a convenience revolution on the surface might actually be a value shift underneath. We didn't just get faster apps and shorter shipping times. We got shorter attention spans, thinner social connections, and buildings designed to crumble in 30 years.

And at the center of it all is money. Not just what we spend. What we save. What we build with. What we expect from the future.

Most people don't think about what money actually is. But it matters because not all money is created equal.

Hard money is money that's difficult to create or increase in supply. It stays valuable over time because no one can make more of it easily. Gold is the classic example. It's rare, durable, and takes real effort to mine and refine. Another example, Bitcoin, is also hard money. Its supply is limited by code, and no one, not even its creator, can produce more than the fixed amount of 21 million.

Soft money, or easy money, is the opposite. It's money that's easy to create. Seashells were once used as money in coastal communities, until outsiders arrived with boatloads of shells and flooded the supply. Today's fiat currencies, like the dollar or euro, can be created by governments with the push of a button. That doesn't make them worthless, but it does mean they tend to lose purchasing power over time.

When people live in a system built on hard money, they tend to think long-term. They save, they build things to last, they plan for future generations. But in a soft money system, the incentives shift. It makes more sense to spend than save, to build cheap and fast rather than strong and slow.

That difference between money that holds value and money that leaks it might sound subtle. But it changes how we live. Money used to be slow. Gold was heavy. Land was sacred. Things were made to last. Then money became paper. Then digits. Then inflation. Then debt. And when the money became fast, so did everything else. This book is going to tell the story of how that happened, and what we might rediscover if we slowed it all down again. Not out of nostalgia. But out of hope. Because maybe the problem isn't just that the world sped up. Maybe it's that we also lost our ability to wait.

Chapter 2: The Sugar High

What is Time Preference?

In 1972, a group of children were brought into a room at Stanford University. Each was offered a marshmallow. They could eat it now or wait fifteen minutes and get two. Some ate it right away. Others squirmed, distracted themselves, and held out. The ones who waited were later found to do better in school, have more stable relationships, and even earn more money.

That simple test, now famous, wasn't really about marshmallows. It was about time preference; a term economists use to describe how much a person values the present versus the future.

High time preference means you want something now, even if it costs you later. It's a lot like chasing a sugar high: briefly satisfying but not built to last. It means you start to crave instant gratification and become conditioned to expect rewards without delay.

Low time preference means you're willing to wait for a bigger payoff. It's a concept that explains a lot more than patience. It explains savings rates, health habits, cultural depth, and even why some civilizations last and others crumble.

But here's the key insight: time preference isn't just personal. It's shaped by the environment around us. And that includes the kind of money we use.

In a world where money loses value over time, why wait? Why save? Why build for the long term when the currency you're saving in is designed to erode? Fiat money systems which are built on inflation, nudge entire societies toward high time preference thinking. The incentives shift. Suddenly, consuming beats saving. Fast beats slow. Cheap beats durable. We slowly become addicted to that pesky short-term sugar high.

We don't just see short-term thinking in spending habits; it even spills over into housing, art, politics, music, education, and even parenting. We live in a culture where the future feels unstable, so the present becomes everything.

But in hard money systems, where money holds or increases its value over time, the opposite happens. People save. They invest in things that take years to mature. They build homes they intend their great-grandchildren to live in. They start projects that may not finish in their lifetime. And they're not saints for doing so. They're just responding to better incentives.

One famous example of low time preference in action is found in the medieval construction of cathedrals. The Cologne Cathedral in Germany began construction in 1248 and wasn't completed until 1880, over 600 years later. Generations of builders, architects, and stone masons worked on something they knew they'd never see finished. Why? Because their society believed in laying stones that would support lives hundreds of years into the future. The money that supported these efforts, typically backed by gold or stable trade made it possible to plan in centuries, not seasons.

Can you imagine people today starting a building project that won't be finished for 600 years?

That kind of patience and belief in the future feels almost impossible in our world of instant results.

Time preference may be one of the most powerful forces shaping our lives, and we rarely stop to think about where it comes from.

In the next chapters, we'll zoom out even further and see how entire eras of human history were defined by whether time was treated as something sacred, or something to be spent.

Chapter 3: Money, Gold, and Trust

We often take money for granted. Most people rarely stop to consider what it truly is, where it originates, or why it holds value. Yet, money isn't a natural object, it's a shared belief, a social construct that functions because we collectively agree on its worth. Throughout history, money has assumed various forms: stones, shells, metals, paper, digital numbers in your bank account, and now digital assets like Bitcoin.

Some skeptics question the legitimacy of digital currencies like Bitcoin by saying, "How can it be money if you can't touch it?" However, this overlooks a fundamental reality of our current financial system: **approximately 90% of the world's money exists solely in digital form**, residing on computer systems and servers. **Only about 10% is physical currency, such as coins and banknotes**. In this light, the idea of a digital form of money isn't as far-fetched as it may seem. If 90% of global money is already digital, how big of a leap would it really be to get closer to 100%?

Before there were coins or paper, there was trust.

In ancient Mesoamerica, the Mayans and Aztecs used cocoa beans as money. A turkey might cost 200 cocoa beans, while a tamale could be had for just a few. Over time, people began to counterfeit the cocoa beans, filling empty shells with dirt to pass them off as real. This subtle erosion of trust slowly undermined the entire system. It's a reminder that sound money isn't just about scarcity, it's about shared confidence.

In parts of Africa today, people use mobile phone credits like money. Minutes are exchanged for groceries, taxi rides, and even rent. It's not printed. It's not minted. But it works, because it's limited, trusted, and convenient. And it shows that money has always adapted to the environment, as long as it meets certain criteria: scarce, transferable, and believed in. These weren't just currencies. They were systems of long-term memory.

Hard money — money that is scarce, stable, and hard to produce, created the foundation for trust. When the money was reliable, people could plan. When it held value, people could save. And when it required effort to create, it demanded responsibility from those who used it.

Gold in particular wasn't just a shiny metal. It was the bedrock of trust. Not because governments said so, but because gold had natural properties that made it universally accepted: durability, divisibility, scarcity, and beauty. It was the closest thing humans had to a timeless store of value.

These systems weren't perfect. They could be manipulated. Wars were still fought. Empires still collapsed. But overall, hard money tended to align individual and societal incentives toward long-term thinking.

Contrast that with money that can be created at will, like the United States Dollar, the Chinese Yuan, or the Japanese Yen. When we use money that is easy to make more of, we hinder our decision-making process. We begin to choose a sugar high based on easy money when we should be making tough decisions about the future. Instead of choosing to prioritize one thing over the other, we simply print more money and choose both options. This leads to a world built on unstable foundations, short-term thinking, and commitments that are unlikely to be kept.

Civilizations that used hard money on the other hand, built pyramids, temples, aqueducts, and libraries that could withstand the test of time. The money they used incentivized creating with a long term vision in mind.

One story that illustrates this contrast comes from 18th-century West Africa. Cowrie shells were used as money across large trade networks. But when European traders began importing vast quantities of cowries from the Indian Ocean, the supply exploded. Suddenly, what had once been scarce became abundant, and its value collapsed. The result wasn't just inflation. People who had saved in shells saw their wealth evaporate. Trade became unstable. Trust broke down.

The Mayans and Aztecs we spoke of earlier, saw stability collapse when fake cocoa beans were produced. Even thousands of years ago, societies understood that when trust in the money breaks down, so does the ability to trade.

It's a reminder that money has never been about what it's made of. It's always been about what we believe in collectively.

This isn't nostalgia. It's a pattern, and it has very real modern impacts. In the next chapters, we'll see how the money we use affects not just architecture and cities, but in how we create, consume, and connect with one another.

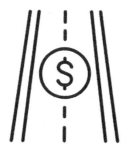

Chapter 4:
Fiat and the Fast Lane

In 1971, something subtle but important changed. President Nixon ended the U.S. dollar's convertibility into gold, quietly cutting the last tie between money and something finite. From that moment on, dollars were no longer backed by anything scarce, they were backed by trust.

Before that, you could exchange dollars for a fixed amount of gold. That connection created a natural limit on how much money could exist. Once it was removed, money became unanchored.

This new system is called fiat money. "Fiat" comes from Latin, meaning "let it be done", or more directly, "forced." Fiat money has value because the government declares it and the people accept it.

To be fair, fiat money has brought a lot of benefits. It helped fuel growth, recovery, innovation, and infrastructure. It gave governments flexibility to respond to emergencies, invest in progress, and expand access to global markets. But it also made money easier to create. And over time, that changed everything.

When money is no longer tied to something scarce like gold, there's no natural limit to how much can be made. Governments and central banks can inject new money into the system with the stroke of a key. And while this can help in the short term, it quietly melts away the value of the money people already hold.

That's inflation. The money still looks the same, but it buys less. And over time, that shift affects behavior. People start spending instead of saving. They borrow more. They plan less. They build faster and cheaper. Not because they want to, but because the system encourages it.

The rise of fiat money didn't just change how economies function. It changed how people think. It shifted time preferences. It rewired incentives.

Today, the average consumer doesn't expect a home to last a lifetime. Developers build for turnover. Products are designed to break. Finance is optimized for speed. Culture is driven by a "give-it-to-me-now" mindset.

Fiat money helped build the modern world. But it may also be why it feels like so much of that world is built on sand.

In the next chapter, we'll see how these changes have manifested in physical form, affecting the homes we live in, the cities we walk through, and how their construction style gives insight into the way we value time.

Chapter 5:
Build Fast, Break Faster

Drive through most suburbs built in the last twenty years and you'll likely see a pattern: homes that look big on the outside but are made with thin walls, hollow doors, and cheap materials. Aesthetically pleasing, structurally temporary.

Compare that to many of the homes built a century ago, often using brickwork, stone foundations, and intricate craftsmanship that still holds up after decades of use. You might not find this everywhere, but if you look carefully, you can surely spot a growing trend.

If you go even further back, you will find even greater craftsmanship in the form of castles, cathedrals, and ancient cities, many of which are still standing.

This isn't just about reminiscing on the past. It's about understanding how our time preferences have physically changed the world we live in.

When people expect the future to be stable, they build things meant to last. When money holds value over time, it makes sense to invest in quality. But when everything feels like it's changing; like prices, policies, and priorities, then the smart move is to build cheap things, sell fast, and move on.

You can see the difference in cities, too. In 19th-century Paris, entire neighborhoods were redesigned by Georges-Eugène Haussmann. His buildings were made from limestone, with iron balconies, high ceilings, and uniform façades. They weren't built for the next quarter; they were built for the next century. Many are still among the most desirable properties in the city. Why? Because they were built when longevity and legacy were the measures for success, not speed and quick profit.

Modern construction often tells a different story. Developers respond to incentives. So do homeowners. If a home is just an investment to flip, why build it like it's going to last 100 years? If you're not rewarded for quality, you focus on quantity. If the value of money is falling, time becomes your enemy.

This mindset isn't limited to houses. It shows up in commercial buildings, strip malls, chain stores, even office towers. Form follows finance.

When the money isn't built to last, neither are the things we build with it.

But it wasn't always this way. During periods of "sound money" when currencies were backed by something scarce like gold, people planned in generations, not quarters. They built homes to raise families in, not to speculate on and make a quick buck. Cities were designed for legacy, not for constant turnover.

There are exceptions today, of course. Not everyone builds disposable. But the broader trend is clear: the faster the money, the more temporary the structures.

And this has cultural consequences. A society surrounded by short-lived buildings begins to internalize the idea that everything is short-lived. Commitments weaken. Care decays. The future becomes abstract.

To build something beautiful and lasting requires more than vision, it requires the belief that the future is worth it. And that belief becomes much harder to sustain when the money you're saving, spending, and earning doesn't share those same long term convictions.

In the next chapter, we'll look at how this shift toward a quick and fast mindset has reshaped our art, and what it means when even beauty itself is put on a timer.

Chapter 6: Art Without Time

In the ages of hard money, art was a long game. Michelangelo spent years painting the ceiling of the Sistine Chapel. Leonardo da Vinci poured his life into The Last Supper, The Mona Lisa, and many other works that weren't rushed, but rather refined over time. They came from a culture that valued patience, craftsmanship, and legacy.

Think about it: Beethoven, Bach, and da Vinci were the most celebrated artists of their time, all creating during eras of relative monetary stability. Fast forward to recent periods: Pollock, Basquiat, Warhol, and much of modern pop art and music emerged during periods of high inflation and fast money.

Can you spot the difference in what society celebrates during low-inflation eras versus high-inflation ones?

It's the difference between Beethoven's Fifth Symphony, which took a long time to compose and endured for centuries, and a pop star's fifth single this month, optimized for streaming but forgotten by next Friday.

It's the difference between masters who spent years on a single canvas, and a banana duct-taped to a wall selling for six figures at an art event. (Yes, this happened).

Our artistic abilities haven't necessarily changed, but the kind of creativity we reward, and the time we allow for it, absolutely has.

Hard money systems, like those backed by gold, provided a stable foundation that encouraged long-term thinking and the desire to invest in works of art and music that lasted for generations. The Renaissance wasn't just a cultural movement; it was underpinned by financial stability that allowed artists and their patrons to focus on legacy rather than immediate returns. Now, imagine a society built on an even harder money than gold, Bitcoin. With its fixed supply and decentralized nature, Bitcoin potentially introduces a level of monetary hardness surpassing that of gold. If gold-backed economies could foster the Renaissance, what cultural and artistic achievements could a Bitcoin-based economy potentially inspire?

This isn't to say Bitcoin guarantees a new Renaissance, but it could open the possibility for one. By encouraging savings over spending and long-term planning over short-term consumption, a Bitcoin based system could cultivate an environment where art, architecture, and culture thrive once again.

Today's art world can still produce brilliance, but the incentives have changed. In an attention economy, going viral often matters more than vision. That duct-taped banana can sell for more than most people's annual salary. A sculpture generated by a design team with help from AI trends online. A song written by a dozen people using data analytics tops the charts.

It's not that good art isn't being made, it is. But the environment doesn't always reward it. When artists are pressured to rush, post constantly, and compete for attention, time disappears from the process. And when time disappears, depth often goes with it.

Art that takes time requires space. Years of training. Confidence in the future. Support from a system that doesn't expect immediate returns.

When the money is fast, the art is too. In a society with high inflation, the art is fast, reactive, and optimized for exposure. One isn't morally better than the other, but they lead to very different outcomes.

The kind of money flowing through a society plays a quiet role in determining which one thrives.

When money is stable, when people save, when we invest in culture, artists can work slowly. They can take risks. They can create for the future, not just for the feed.

That doesn't mean everyone can easily become an artist in a world of hard money, quite the opposite. Only those truly destined for the profession would thrive as the open market relentlessly chooses those great artists who are worthy of becoming the voices of a generation.

Hard money doesn't automatically make good art. But it makes time possible. And time makes quality possible.

Art is one of the most sensitive indicators of a culture's time horizon. If all we're making is fast, forgettable, disposable work, what does that say about how we view the future?

In the next chapter, we'll turn our attention to another time-intensive domain, war. And ask what happens when governments can finance conflict with money they don't yet have.

Chapter 7: War & Waste

War has always come with a price. But the way that price is paid, and when, has changed dramatically over time.

In times of hard money, wars came with real limits. Armies had to be paid in gold, not in promises or printed currency. Debt couldn't be pushed off forever, it had to be repaid. And when the gold ran out, the war usually did too.

In 1812, Napoleon's war into Russia was ambitious, but unsustainable. As his army pushed deeper into foreign territory, the cost of maintaining supply lines ballooned. France's treasury, backed by metal and grain, began to strain under the pressure. When winter set in and resources ran low, the campaign collapsed, not just because of snow, but because the money ran out. The war ended not with a peace treaty, but with a retreat.

This wasn't unique. Throughout history, conflict has often ended when the bill came due. Money, in this way, acted as a natural restraint. It forced leaders to weigh costs against conviction.

But today, that restraint is weaker.

Fiat systems allow governments to fund wars without immediately having the money to pay for them. They can borrow from the future, create currency at scale, and push off the pain. The tab still exists, it's just less visible, and it might be paid for by people not even born yet.

Instead of showing up as higher taxes or public fundraising, the cost of modern conflict often shows up years later. Not as a bill, but as inflation. As national debt. As slowly eroding purchasing power spread across generations.

We see the same reckless patterns of spending, often to the point of weakening a currency, reflected in areas like healthcare, education, and public support programs. These systems are often essential, yet they consistently under-deliver despite massive funding, especially in The United States. The reason for this is clear, when money flows without clear accountability, we lose our sense of direction. And without proper incentives built into our money, we will get distorted outcomes.

Think of a young family trying to save for a home. They set aside money each month, but prices keep rising faster than their savings. Groceries inch up. Gas inches up. Rent creeps higher. They're not making bad decisions; they're simply living inside a system that silently moves the goalposts. They work hard for their money, but the money itself works against them.

That's not a flaw in the family. That's a reflection of the system.

Fiat money stretches time. It lets leaders act quickly, sometimes for good. But it can also allow people in power to avoid hard trade-offs. It removes the friction that used to force clarity.

In hard money systems, decisions had to be measured. You couldn't fund everything. So you prioritized. You made trade-offs. You saved for what mattered most. It wasn't perfect, but it grounded things.

A future with harder money wouldn't be utopian. But it could restore that grounding.

Imagine a world where funding conflicts requires public support and direct financial backing, where decisions carry real financial limits, not just moral ones. In such a world, war might not disappear entirely, but it would likely be far less common.

It would be a world where action requires reflection, because funding must be airtight from the start. Saying yes would mean saying no to something else, not just pressing a button on the money printer.

This chapter isn't an argument against safety nets. Or against action. It's a call for realism. For incentives that reflect what's truly sustainable.

When money is rooted in something scarce, choices begin to reflect that scarcity. And when real choices must be made, outcomes can be more honest, and peace can be seen as a more desirable option.

In the next chapter, we'll explore something that could be reviving that mindset, one that appears to value control, longevity, and a different perspective on the future: Bitcoin.

Chapter 8: Bitcoin

Bitcoin is often misunderstood. People see the headlines, the price charts, the craziness, and they think it's just another fad. And how could you blame them? On the surface their skepticism appears completely justified. But beneath the noise is a deeper possibility: that Bitcoin isn't just a new form of money, somewhat of a financial philosophy. One that could contain the seeds for a new framework of how we value and perceive money on Earth.

To understand why, we first need to understand why money matters at all and how we might be taking the concept of money for granted.

Without money, you would have to trade. You'd need to find someone who wants what you have and has what you want, all at the same time. That's hard to do. Money solves this problem. It lets you trade with anyone, even if you don't want the same things. You do your work, they do theirs, and you can both buy what you need. That's why money matters; it keeps life moving and helps people work together.

Throughout history, societies have used many things as money, from seashells and salt to livestock and beads, to gold and silver, then to government-issued currencies backed by gold. Today, most money is backed by nothing tangible at all, just the authority and promise of a government. When we look at money through a historical lens, we're reminded that what counts as money has been shaped more by collective belief than anything else. It was never the material itself that gives money power, or any specific quality, rather it is the trust people place in it.

But what actually is money?

Well, economists define money as serving three basic roles:

- *Store of Value*
- *Unit of Account*
- *Medium of Exchange*

Store of Value – This is something that holds its worth over time. For example, a gold coin can still buy about the same amount of goods decades later, it keeps its purchasing power. If you save it, its value stays strong. The U.S. dollar, on the other hand, tends to lose value over time, meaning it buys you less each year as prices rise

Unit of Account – This is something we use to measure and compare value. Just like we use inches to measure length or miles per hour to measure speed, we use dollars to measure the value of goods and services. When you see a price tag that says "$4," you instantly know what that means. Dollars make it easy to compare the cost of different things. Today, the U.S. dollar is the most widely used unit of account because it's stable and well understood. But some believe that as Bitcoin becomes more stable over time, it could eventually take on this role as well.

Medium of Exchange – This is something people use to trade. In some parts of the world, Bitcoin is already being used this way. Freelancers get paid in it, and some businesses accept it as payment, especially for online transactions or international deals.

Right now, Bitcoin mostly plays the role of a store of value, especially in countries where local currency is unstable. In some places, it's also used for payments, especially online or across borders. But it's not yet widely used as a unit of account, and its wild price swings still make people cautious.

Some critics say Bitcoin doesn't qualify as money at all. They argue it's not widely accepted, not stable, and not practical for everyday use. And they have a point, adoption is currently limited, especially in daily life.

Still, for others, Bitcoin offers something else that goes beyond definitions of money: a system that doesn't rely on governments or banks. A system built on verification. A system whose rules are baked into code and agreed upon collectively, not manipulated by a select few.

So how does it actually work?

Bitcoin is like a shared digital notebook, a public record of transactions that everyone can see and agree on. Instead of being managed by a government or a bank, it's run by a network of computers around the world. No one owns it, and no single person can change the rules.

New transactions get added by participants called miners. They use computers to solve puzzles that help power the network. As they do so, they're rewarded with Bitcoin. Their computer must reach a consensus with all the other computers, if they help reach the right answer collectively, they are rewarded. If they purposefully try to damage the system and input incorrect information, they will simply end up spending energy while accomplishing nothing. This setup encourages people to keep the system running and honest, because there's a clear reward for doing the right thing, and a cost for trying to cheat.

It's this combination of openness, fairness, and independence that makes Bitcoin so different from the money we're used to.

These characteristics could significantly shift how people perceive money, risk, and time.

In many places, these shifts have already started to take place. Bitcoin has quietly filled a gap: when bank accounts are frozen, when currencies collapse, or when options run out.

In Venezuela, as the Bolívar collapsed, families turned to Bitcoin, not because it was trendy, but because it was survivable. Merchants started pricing goods in Satoshis (Bitcoin's smallest unit). Parents saved Bitcoin on USB drives. Freelancers demanded crypto payments from international clients just to hold on to value.

In the West, it can be difficult to grasp why people in Venezuela would turn to something like Bitcoin. Their urgency to preserve value is far greater than what we experience. But even in the West, more people are beginning to see Bitcoin not just as a speculative asset, but as a serious alternative. For them, it's no longer a gamble, it's a full embrace of what they believe is "good money."

History shows us what "good money" can make possible. It helped spark eras of progress in art, science, architecture, medicine, and peace. At the heart of these eras were a shared belief that the future was worth building for, supported by a stable system based on gold, money that held its value over generations.

Now imagine a society built on something even more scarce than gold. If gold helped inspire the Renaissance, perhaps something akin to a digital form of gold, like Bitcoin, could help spark the next one. And perhaps it could lead to a new kind of prosperity.

Not just financial prosperity, but prosperity rooted in cleaner air, healthier soil, safer food, art and music with greater depth, and more livable communities. These are the kinds of things that are valued more in a society thinking long-term. When we think long term, we change the definition of success to include the well-being of people and the planet, not just profits.

In the next chapter, we will explore a vision of what it might look like to live in a world with reliable money that focuses on the long term.

Chapter 9: Visions of a Slower Future

The city felt different now.

The buildings didn't compete. They stood with quiet confidence, limestone and wood, carefully carved signs, copper rooftops that would age with grace. People didn't rush between the buildings. They walked.

At the corner, a bakery passed down for three generations still made bread by hand. Next door, a tailor pressed a gorgeous suit he'd spent six months sewing, cutting, and refining. And just beyond, a new cathedral was being framed in stone, set to be finished in thirty years.

No one called it old-fashioned. It was just normal life.

Families lived in the same homes for decades, sometimes centuries. And those who desired to move often could do so easily as well. The homes were designed with thick stone walls, immaculate porches where people hung out, and rooms that could be adapted and re-adapted over time. It wasn't uncommon for a child to plant a tree with their grandparents, then read to their own kids beneath its branches.

There were no overnight homes. No "starter" neighborhoods made of plastic and drywall. Even commercial buildings, libraries, public markets, and offices, were constructed to outlast their founders. Architecture school once again included entire semesters on how to make things permanent.

People saved more. They spent with intention. Not because they were minimalists or restrictive, but because their money held its value, and so did the things they bought. There was no rush to keep up with what wouldn't last.

Art flourished, not just because patrons could afford to fund it, but because time allowed for mastery. Musicians spent years perfecting a single composition. Painters, like the Renaissance masters before them, took on commissions that lasted decades and even lifetimes. Patrons paid up front, trusting that great beauty was worth waiting for. Woodworkers signed their pieces not for fame, but so their great-grandchildren would know who built them. And kids didn't dream of going viral, they dreamed of building things worth keeping.

Medicine evolved too. Doctors weren't incentivized to treat symptoms in fifteen-minute slots. They had time to know their patients. Medical schools rewarded diagnostic depth and long-term outcomes. Patients lived longer not just from technology, but because the culture itself supported longevity.

Even technology changed. Devices were repairable. Designed to be used for a decade, not a product cycle. The most admired engineers weren't the ones who moved fast and broke things, but the ones who built things that didn't need to be fixed.

And farming changed too. No longer dominated by industrial mega corporations focused on yield and shelf life, agriculture became smaller, local, and intentional. Small farms returned, not for nostalgia, but because people started valuing nutrition over mass production. Crops were rotated to restore the soil. Fertilizers were replaced by compost. Food wasn't just cheap, it was nourishing. Farmers weren't racing to cut corners. They were building something sustainable, where quality mattered more than volume. Clean food became as valued as clean cars.

People started to care not just about what food cost, but where it came from, how it was grown, and what impact it had on the land. Schools taught soil health alongside math. Parents brought their kids to farmers' markets, not just for groceries, but for lessons in stewardship.

The environment became a central part of the collective thinking. Clean rivers. Thriving ecosystems. Healthy soil. These weren't just environmental goals, they were economic indicators. Success wasn't just about growth anymore. It was about resilience and legacy.

The world wasn't perfect. But it was rooted.

This wasn't a return to the past. It was something new. A world where progress wasn't measured by speed, but by depth. Where wealth wasn't just financial, it was cultural, relational, environmental.

No one called it a low time preference society. Most people had never heard that term. But they felt it. In their neighborhoods, in their food, in their work, in their families.

And it all started when the money slowed down, not because the old system was broken, but because its chapter had closed. Fiat money had fueled expansion, scale, and global access. It had opened doors. But eventually, it asked too much too fast. And when it reached its limit, something better took root.

A world that chose to last.

Maybe the measure of a healthy economy isn't how fast it grows, but how well it sustains over the long term. Maybe it's not in quarterly profits, but in clean rivers, fresh air, rich soil, and nourishing food.

What if economic success looked less like numbers on a screen and more like healthy humans, thriving ecosystems, and a world we're proud to pass on?

Chapter 10: Choosing a Timeline

Picture two futures.

In one, the world keeps going in the same direction. Everything gets faster. Attention spans shrink. Homes get cheaper and flimsier. Art gets louder and emptier. Debt grows. The money loses value year after year. And so do the things built on top of it.

In the other, we slow down. Not because we're

forced to, but because we choose to. Because we desire to build a world with the future in mind.

The question this book has been circling the whole time is this: What kind of timeline do we want to live on?

A fast one burns hot. It rewards now. It optimizes for clicks, shortcuts, and consumption. It leaves us feeling like we are on the tail end of a sugar crash.

A slow one rewards patience. It builds for legacy. It assumes the future matters.

Money isn't the only thing that shapes a society. But it is the foundation. And when the foundation is solid, when the money is hard, fair, and trusted people tend to plant deeper roots.

We've seen this before. In eras of hard money, civilizations built cathedrals, funded masterpieces, raised multi-generational homes, and created systems that lasted. In eras of easy money, things tend to come and go.

Something like Bitcoin could be a spark, an invitation to think differently. It reminds us that money can be something more than a system of spending. It can be a system that amplifies the best qualities of humanity.

And that means the future doesn't have to be fast to be good. It can be beautiful, durable, and worth waiting for.

The choice isn't between the past and the present.

It's between Fast Money & Fast Times, or something better.

In the next chapter we will explore how these cultural changes begin at the individual level, often with how we earn, save, and spend.

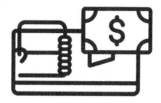

Chapter 11: The Cost of Now

High time preference doesn't always show up in obvious ways. You don't need to be reckless or impulsive to fall into short-term thinking. In fact, some of the most common financial mistakes happen quietly, through everyday decisions, habits, and assumptions that add up over time.

Let's take a look at a few familiar patterns.

The first of these short-term thinking habits is living one raise ahead

You get a raise. Instead of saving it, you upgrade your car. Or move into a slightly bigger apartment. Or take on a new subscription or service that used to feel "extra."

This is known as lifestyle inflation, when your expenses rise with your income. It's not always intentional. Sometimes it's just a default response to "more." But over time, it can prevent real wealth from building, because every dollar that comes in goes right back out.

Another common pattern is the "buy now, worry later" mentality.

Credit cards, zero-interest financing, buy-now-pay-later apps, these tools can be convenient. But they can also encourage present-moment gratification at the expense of long-term security. You're not necessarily buying more than you can afford. You're just buying it now instead of saving up and buying it later. The actual price? Interest, stress, or just the quiet burden of always being behind.

Then there's the challenge of emergency-free living.

Only about 4 in 10 Americans can cover a $1,000 emergency with savings. That's not because people are lazy or bad with money. It's often because they've never been taught to expect the unexpected. In a high time preference world, the future is blurry. So, planning for it feels optional. But the truth is: if you don't plan for emergencies, emergencies might be planning for you.

Finally, there's the monthly mentality.

Many people don't think in years, they think in months, and that is completely understandable. Rent, utilities, car payments, phone bills. Everything is framed around the next due date. But that mindset makes it hard to zoom out. It makes it harder to set aside money for future goals, because the present always feels louder.

None of these behaviors mean that you have failed. They're simply the result of a system that often encourages short-term thinking. When the money you earn is losing value to inflation, saving can feel pointless, whether we are conscious of it or not. When costs keep rising, it's hard to imagine "getting ahead." And when social media constantly shows the highlight reel of others' lives, there's subtle pressure to keep up, even if it comes at the cost of your future.

But understanding this isn't about guilt. It's about clarity.

Because there's another way to think about money. Not as a game of survival, but hopefully as a tool to provide a beautiful life for oneself and their loved ones.

When you spend less than you earn, you buy flexibility. When you save for the future, you reduce fear. When you invest in things that grow slowly but steadily, you give yourself a longer runway and a bigger perspective.

None of these things happen overnight. But they start with mindset.

In a world driven by fast money, stillness can feel countercultural. But as the pace of life accelerates, stillness becomes a kind of power. It's what allows decisions to become more deliberate. Ideas to sharpen. Creativity to deepen. And priorities to realign with long-term goals.

A shift toward harder money isn't just a financial change, it has the potential to change how we live. It invites less urgency, more presence. Less reactivity, more intention. In this kind of environment, we're no longer forced to chase what's next, we're able to build what lasts.

This is what a lower time preference really looks like in practice. It's not austerity or denial. It's choosing the long view. Building for the future even when the present is screaming for attention. It's the difference between eating that marshmallow now, or saving it, planting it, growing a tree, and eating two marshmallows later. (The marshmallow probably wouldn't grow into a tree, but let's go with it for now.)

In the next chapter, we'll zoom in on where time preference gets shaped most profoundly: education and parenting.

Chapter 12: Teaching the Future

If you want to understand how a society thinks about time, look at how it teaches its children.

Schools are more than buildings. They're time machines. They prepare kids for the future or train them to react to the present. Today, many education systems reflect the same short-term incentives we see elsewhere. Test scores are prioritized over curiosity. Speed is valued over depth. Standardized answers replace independent thought.

The structure of modern schooling didn't arise by accident. It was built during the industrial age to produce efficient workers for a predictable economy. That's why the focus often centers on memorization, performance, and compliance. But the world is no longer predictable, and the economy is anything but stable.

Kids today are growing up in a world where college is more expensive than ever, careers are less linear, technology evolves faster than school curriculums, and financial literacy is rarely taught at all. We've handed them a system designed for the past, then asked them to navigate the future with it.

And it's not just schools shaping that mindset. It's found in homes and parenting styles.

In today's culture, many parents feel immense pressure to keep up, enrolling their children in countless activities, managing every detail, and staying ahead of every trend. Childhood has become a schedule. Play has become structured. Even rest time feels "optimized".

That pressure comes from love, but also from a broader cultural anxiety: the fear of falling behind. The fear of not doing "enough." Yet what children may need most isn't more stimulation, it's more space. Space to be bored. To explore. To build. To wonder.

Parenting with a low time preference doesn't mean strict routines or hyper-discipline. It means planting values that take years to bear fruit. Teaching the importance of delaying gratification. Thinking long-term. Practicing patience. Building for something bigger than oneself. It's about helping children see that value isn't always immediate, and that some of the best things in life are the ones you wait for.

Because financial systems shape more than just wallets. They shape worldviews.

When money loses value, so does patience. When schools and homes reflect that same urgency, children learn to live on fast-forward. But what if education taught endurance? What if parenting modeled peace instead of pressure? What if kids were raised not just to succeed in the system, but to question it, improve it, and build something better?

In the next chapter, we'll summarize possible goals for the future of finance and for the world.

Chapter 13:
The Final Goal

Throughout this journey, we've examined how our perceptions of time and money influence every part of our lives. The way we build our homes, raise our children, and plan for the future, are all deeply shaped by the economic structures around us. At the center of those structures is the money we use — currently designed in a way that favors speed over longevity.

In a world driven by fiat currency, where money can be created at will, there's a subtle yet pervasive shift in values. The easy creation of money encourages rapid consumption, short-term investments, and a culture of disposability. We see it in the transient nature of modern architecture, the fleeting trends in art and fashion, and the emphasis on standardized testing over critical thinking in education.

This acceleration doesn't just affect our institutions; it permeates our personal lives. The constant push for productivity leaves little room for reflection. Decisions are made hastily, often sacrificing quality and sustainability for speed and convenience. The result is a society that moves quickly but often lacks direction, a culture rich in information but poor in wisdom.

Yet, change is possible. By re-evaluating our relationship with money and time, we can begin to shift our focus from the immediate to the enduring. Embracing systems that value scarcity and stability can encourage behaviors that prioritize long-term benefits over short-term gains. This doesn't mean rejecting progress but rather aligning it with purpose and foresight.

Imagine communities where buildings are constructed to last generations, where education fosters curiosity and resilience, and where economic decisions are made with an eye toward future impact. In such a world, patience becomes a virtue, and investments, whether in infrastructure, relationships, or personal growth, are made with care and intention.

This vision isn't a distant utopia; it's a tangible possibility that begins with individual choices. By adopting a mindset that values the long term, we lay the groundwork for a more stable, thoughtful, and fulfilling society. It's about moving beyond the cycle of instant gratification and towards a culture that honors the time-tested principles of diligence, integrity, and stewardship.

In embracing the long game, we don't just alter our economic models; we transform our collective outlook. We shift from a story of relentless hurrying to one of deliberate progress. And in doing so, we create a legacy defined by purpose, longevity, and meaning.

Because in a world shaped by fast money and fast times, it's easy to lose sight of what truly matters.

To build things that last.
To instill curiosity in our children.
To create art that's rooted in meaning.
To grow relationships that feel connected.
To navigate life with care, choosing peace when we can.

And above all, to leave behind a world we're proud to pass on to future generations.

Author's Biography

Max Matles is a Certified Financial Planner™ and tax professional based in Orange County, California. He works at Matles Wealth Management alongside his father, David, who has been in the financial planning industry since 1998, the same year Max was born.

Max's path into finance started early. He grew up surrounded by the family business and officially entered the profession in 2019 after earning his first license. He completed his bachelor's degree at Grand Canyon University in 2022, became a Certified Financial Planner™ in 2023, and earned his Enrolled Agent designation in 2024, a federal credential that allows him to represent taxpayers in court and file tax returns across all 50 states.

Outside of his professional work, Max has a wide range of interests. He is passionate about extreme sports like rock climbing, slacklining (tightrope walking), and long-distance running. He also creates art and has a deep appreciation for movement, nature, and physical challenges that demand focus and presence. Max's fascination with Bitcoin and blockchain technology began in high school. Later, while studying in college, he launched a small Bitcoin mining operation out of his dorm room, recruiting a few friends to help and taking advantage of what they referred to as "free" university electricity. Max convinced the boys that the high cost of college tuition was enough to justify mining for Bitcoin. With his encouragement, they set off on the mining experiment, equal parts hustle, curiosity, and mischief.

The setup ran without issue until the school flagged an unusually high electric bill coming from a single dorm and eventually shut the project down. New rules were put in place just for Max. Today, it's a humorous story, but one that points to Max's early instinct for understanding systems, incentives, and the future of finance.

In 2018, Max discovered Vipassana meditation and the teachings of the Buddha, which sparked a deep inner transformation. He developed a strong daily meditation practice and began to see the profound impact of a life devoted to cultivating inner peace.

Max spent several years considering the monastic path and planning to ordain as a Buddhist monk.

Ultimately, Max found that serving others through financial planning offered a powerful way to live out the same principles, cultivating inner peace, serving others, and developing the mind, the same practices he once sought through the monastic path. In the end he discovered helping others find peace brought him closer to his own.

GET IN TOUCH WITH MAX

Do you have questions, comments, or would you like to get in contact with Max?

max@matles.com

MAXMATLES.COM

714-697-1998

May your life be filled with peace and joy...

Made in the USA
Monee, IL
07 August 2025

22057330R00056